15710

ITALY

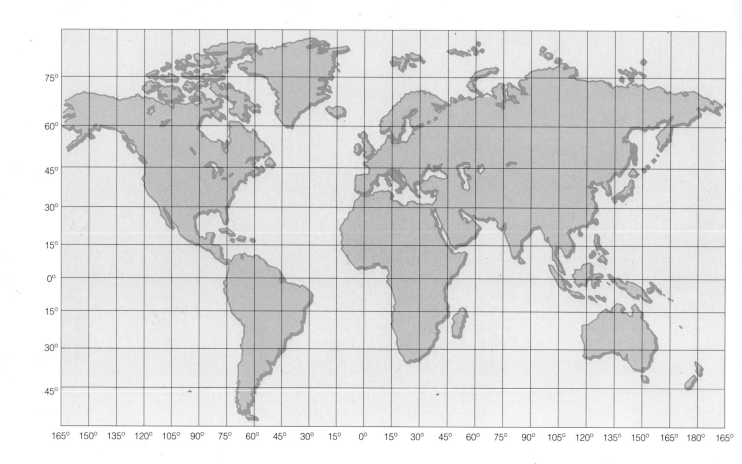

ITALY

Derek Allen

RAINTREE STECK-VAUGHN
PUBLISHERS

Austin, Texas

Published by Raintree Steck-Vaughn Publishers, an imprint of
Steck-Vaughn Company

Design	Roger Kohn
Editors	Diana Russell, Shirley Shalit
DTP editor	Helen Swansbourne
Picture research	Valerie Mulcahy
Illustration	János Márffy
Consultant	Marco Ausenda
Commissioning editor	Debbie Fox

We are grateful to the following for permission
to reproduce photographs:
Front Cover: Paul Mulcahy *above,* Zefa *below;*
Andes Press Agency, page 18 (Vincenzo Serra); Cephas Picture Library,
page 29 (Mick Rock); 1995 Comstock,
pages 16 (Julian Nieman), 36 *above*; Granata Press Service, pages 11
below (Filmgo), 13 *left* (Patrizio Morandi), 14 *above* (Tessore), 22 *above*
(Lomonaco), 23 (Ken Welsh), 28/29 (Vincenzo Signorelli), 30, 36 *below*
(Andrea Strianese), 38 *below* (Enzo Signorelli), 40 *below* (Guiseppe
Salomone), 41 (Flavio Catalano); Robert Harding Picture Library, pages 10,
27 (Mike Newton); The Hutchison Library, page 22 *below* (Julia Davey);
The Image Bank, pages 24 *below* (Guido Alberto Rossi), 37 (Giuliano
Colliva); Magnum, pages 17 (Raymond Depardon), 42 (Richard Kalvar);
Richard Newton, page 31; Rex Features, pages 14 *below*, 21 (SIPA), 24
above (SIPA/P Schwartz), 25 (Roberto Koch), 32 and 33 (SIPA/A Cavalli);
Spectrum, pages 8 *above* and *below,* 11 *above,* 39; Frank Spooner
Pictures, pages 28 *left* (GAMMA/Eduardo Fornaciari), 35 (Marescot
Virgnaud), 38 *above* (Luigi Tazzari), 43 (GAMMA/Raphael Gillarde);
Tony Stone Images, pages 20 (Mike Caldwell), 26 (Chris Windsor); Sygma,
13 *right* (Alberto Pizzoli), 28 *right* (J P Amet); TRIP, pages 9 (J Bartos),
12 (Overseas/Mario Lanfranchi), 19 (Helene Rogers), 34 (Reinaldo
Vargas), 40 *above* (Overseas/V Pigazzini).

The statistics given in this book are the most up to date available at the
time of going to press

Printed in Hong Kong by Wing King Tong

1 2 3 4 5 6 7 8 9 0 PO 99 98 97 96 95

Library of Congress Cataloging-in-Publication Data
Allen, Derek, 1959–
Italy / Derek Allen.
p. cm. — (Country fact files)
Includes bibliographical references and index.
Summery: Examines the landscape, climate, weather, population, culture,
and industries of Italy.
ISBN 0-8114-6196-3
1. Italy – Juvenile literature. (1. Italy)
I. Title. II. Series.
DG417.A58 1996
914.5–dc20
95-30687
CIP AC

C
O
N
T
E
N
T
S

Words that are explained in the glossary are printed in
SMALL CAPITALS the first time they are mentioned in the text.

■ INTRODUCTION

For 900 years from the end of the 6th century B.C., Italy was ruled by the Romans, who established an empire that stretched from Britain to Africa. Their influence can still be seen today in the alphabet, the languages, and even the legal systems of Western countries.

After the Roman Empire ended, Italy was

▲ **Built in Rome between A.D. 70 and 72, the Colosseum is a reminder of Italy's immense historical and cultural heritage.**

◄ **The Victor Emmanuel Gallery in Milan houses an impressive collection of shops, selling all sorts of luxury items to wealthy Italians and foreign visitors.**

► **Poverty is still a problem in areas to the south of Italy and on the islands of Sardinia and Sicily. Basic services, such as hospitals, clinics, and communications systems, here are poor. People's incomes are low.**

invaded by foreign powers and broken up into separate states. Italian influence was once more important during the RENAISSANCE, when the country was Europe's center of art and learning. But more foreign invasions followed. The Italian states were only unified as one country in 1861.

The 20th century has brought great changes. Industrialization began in the early 1900s, later than in other European countries. In 1922, a FASCIST government came to power, and led the country to defeat in World War II. After the war, a DEMOCRATIC republic was set up and a new era began.

Today, Italy has a highly developed economy, although the north remains much richer than the more agricultural south,

ITALY AT A GLANCE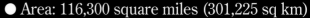

- Area: 116,300 square miles (301,225 sq km)
- Population: 58,138,000
- Population density: 499 people per square mile (192 people per sq km)
- Capital: Rome, population 2.69 million
- Other main cities: Milan 1.4 million; Naples 1.054 million; Turin 1 million; Palermo 731,418; Genoa 706,754; Bologna 417,410; Florence 413,000
- Highest mountain: Monte Bianco, 15,521 feet (4,731 m)
- Longest river: Po, 391 miles (652 km)
- Language: Italian
- Major religion: Christianity
- Life expectancy: 73.5 years for men; 80 for women
- Currency: Italian lira, written as L. (The plural is lire)
- Economy: Highly industrialized. Agriculture is declining
- Major resources: Methane gas, hydro-electricity
- Major products: Machinery and transportation equipment, textiles, clothing, food, tourism, financial services
- Environmental problems: air and water pollution from domestic and industrial waste, soil erosion, loss of wild areas

known as the MEZZOGIORNO. Italian cars such as Fiat and Ferrari are exported all over the world, as are clothes produced by companies like Benetton and Gucci. Tourism is also thriving — millions of people from all over the world visit the country every year to enjoy its varied scenery and its art treasures.

In this book, you will find out about the country, its people, their way of life, and what Italy can expect the future to bring.

THE LANDSCAPE

Italy covers an area of 116,314 square miles (301,252 sq km). It measures about 780 miles (1,300 km) from north to south, and (excluding the long northern border area) some 150 miles (250 km) from east to west.

Two important mountain regions dominate the landscape. In the north, the rugged Alps form a natural frontier with four countries: France, Switzerland, Austria, and Slovenia. The more rolling Apennines run down the middle of the Italian PENINSULA to Sicily. There are also lower mountains in Sardinia. More than three-quarters of the whole country is classified as hilly or mountainous.

The longest river is the Po, which flows eastward for 390 miles (652 km) over the

▲ *Characteristic farmhouses built among the gently rolling hills of Tuscany.*

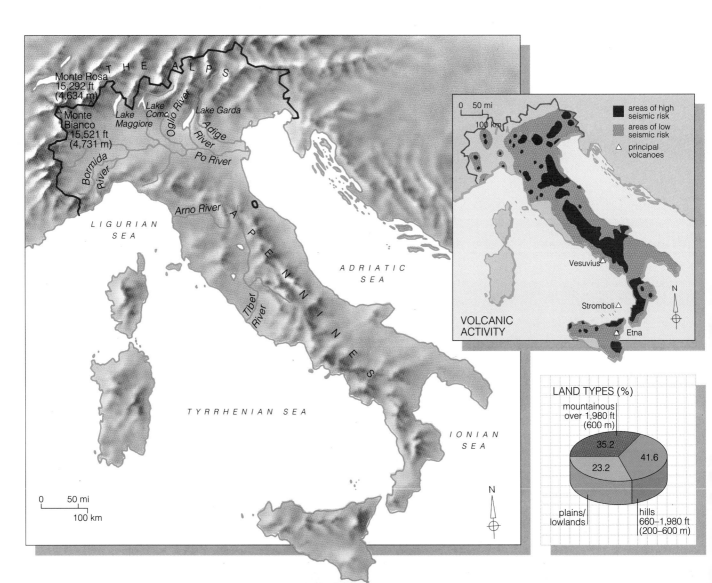

KEY FACTS

● More than 120,000 people have been killed by earthquakes in Italy since 1900.
● The Italian coastline is 4,660 mi (7,500 km) long.
● Forests cover 22% of the country, compared with 25–30% cover in France and Germany, 30% in the U.S., and up to 60% in northern European countries.

▼ *The Po Delta: branches of water spread out in a triangle shape along flat, fertile land before entering the Adriatic Sea.*

▲ *The harbor of Portofino, built on the rugged coastline of eastern Liguria in northern Italy.*

northern plains to the Adriatic Sea. The Po River Valley makes up more than a quarter of the country's lowlands. Other rivers include the Tiber, which flows for 211 miles (352 km) from the Apennines to the Mediterranean, passing through Rome. Italy also has 1,500 lakes. The largest are Garda, Maggiore, and Como in the north of the country.

Sicily and Sardinia, which together make up 98% of Italy's island territory, are the largest islands in the Mediterranean. Other famous Italian islands include Capri and Ischia, situated near Naples.

Another feature of Italy's landscape is that some areas are at risk of earthquakes. There are also four active volcanoes in the south of the country, including Vesuvius, near Naples, and Etna, near Catania in Sicily. Etna's most recent eruption was in 1992.

CLIMATE AND WEATHER

Since Italy is almost the same distance from the Equator and the North Pole, much of the country has a mild climate. But there are regional differences, because of factors such as how mountainous an area is, and how near it is to the sea.

There are six basic climatic regions. In the north, the Alpine area has brief, cool summers and long, cold winters. Heavy snowfalls and below freezing temperatures are common. By contrast, the lower Po Valley region enjoys hot summers, with temperatures sometimes exceeding 86°F (30°C), although winters are cold and foggy. Rain here falls mostly in spring and autumn.

The Apennine region in the middle of the country is warm in the summer and cold in the winter, with an average annual temperature range of 32°–68°F (0°–20°C). Along the western coastal Tyrrhenian–Ligurian region, mild winters are followed by pleasantly hot summers. There is little rainfall, and snow is almost unknown. Along

▲ *Vacationers at Riserva dello Zingaro on Capri. Warm sea temperatures mean that people go swimming here even in midwinter.*

KEY FACTS

● The cold, dry, winter wind known as the Bora can reach speeds of up to 120 mph (200 kph).

● In November 1994, heavy rains in northern Italy led to floods that killed 63 people and left more than 10,000 homeless.

● In 1987–91, the total percentage of sunshine hours in Cagliari, Sardinia, was 56.5%.

● In 1988–92, the average maximum yearly temperature in Catania, Sicily, was 76°F (24.4°C). This compares with averages of 63°F (17.1°C) for Turin, and 64.4°F (18°C) for Milan.

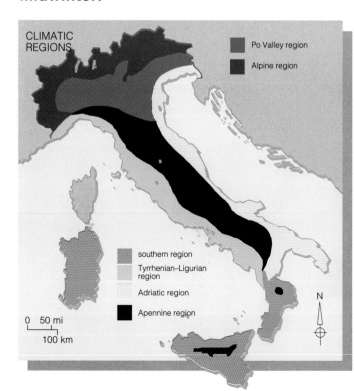

CLIMATIC REGIONS

Po Valley region
Alpine region

southern region
Tyrrhenian–Ligurian region
Adriatic region
Apennine region

0   50 mi
100 km

N

the eastern coast, however, the Adriatic region experiences winters that can be up to 9°F (5°C) colder. This area is exposed to cold, northerly, winter winds called the BORA.

Finally, the southern region (including Sicily and Sardinia) enjoys a more typically Mediterranean climate, with very mild winters, averaging around 52°F (11°C), and hot summers, up to 95°F (35°C). Annual rainfall here averages only 18.4 inches (460 mm) so drought can be a problem.

▲A ski lift near Cervinia in the northern Alps. Heavy snowfalls usually occur in December, and skiing has become extremely popular.

▲Since 1900, the city of Venice has sunk 9 inches (23 cm), and springtime flooding due to the "acqua alta" (high water) has become increasingly common.

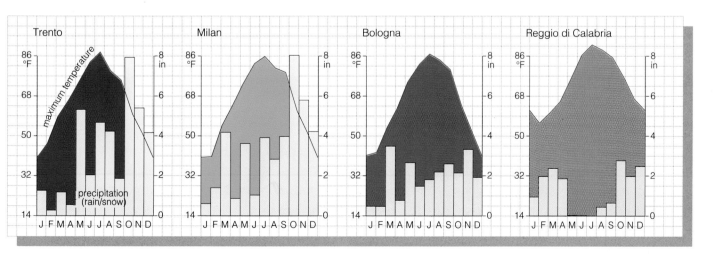

■■ NATURAL RESOURCES

◄ *Adrano, near Catania in Italy, is the site of the only solar energy plant operating in a European Union country.*

▼ *Marble quarries in Carrara, Tuscany. Italian marble is a valuable export. Formerly prized by sculptors, it is now mainly used in the construction industry.*

Although it is a highly industrialized country, Italy's energy resources are limited and expensive to extract. The coal mines in Sardinia are gradually being shut down as they are not economical, while domestic oil production — mainly from oil wells in Sicily — accounts for only 5% of the country's present needs. Imports of coal and oil now make up approximately 80% of Italy's energy requirements, and 56% of the total spent on energy.

Methane gas is an important source of energy in the country. There are deposits in the Po Valley and the province of Ravenna, and beneath the Adriatic Sea, providing one-fifth of national energy needs, but they are fast being used up. Italy imports additional quantities via pipelines from Algeria and Ukraine.

Hydroelectric power (HEP) is another major energy source, particularly in the Alpine regions. In the 1960s, HEP accounted for 80% of national energy production, but today its share has fallen to

25%. There are plans to expand HEP output in the future.

Alternative energy sources are being investigated. Organic refuse-burning plants were set up in the area around Florence at the end of the 1980s as a possible solution to future energy problems, and a major solar energy center has been established in Sicily. Wind power is a more difficult

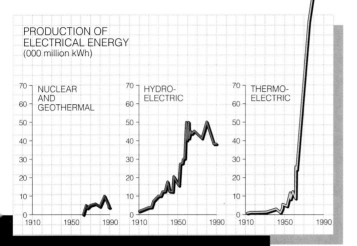

PRODUCTION OF
ELECTRICAL ENERGY
(000 million kWh)

NUCLEAR
AND
GEOTHERMAL

HYDRO-
ELECTRIC

THERMO-
ELECTRIC

alternative, as it is hard to find areas with
suitably consistent climatic conditions.

Italy's chief mineral resource is stone
deposits. The most important marble
quarries are in the Veneto region and
Tuscany. Limestone, which is used to make
cement, is found in quarries throughout the
country. There are also deposits of rock salt
in Sicily.

KEY FACTS

● Italy's national energy
requirements totalled
175 billion kilowatts in
1994, compared with just
4.5 billion in 1920.

● Since 1951, an area called
"Metanopoli," near Milan,
has produced vast quantities
of methane gas.

● Italy imports two-fifths of
the lumber it uses.

● The world's largest plant
for the industrial production
of diesel fuel derived from
vegetable products was set
up in Livorno in 1993.

● In a referendum held in
1987, Italians rejected the
idea of developing a nuclear
power industry.

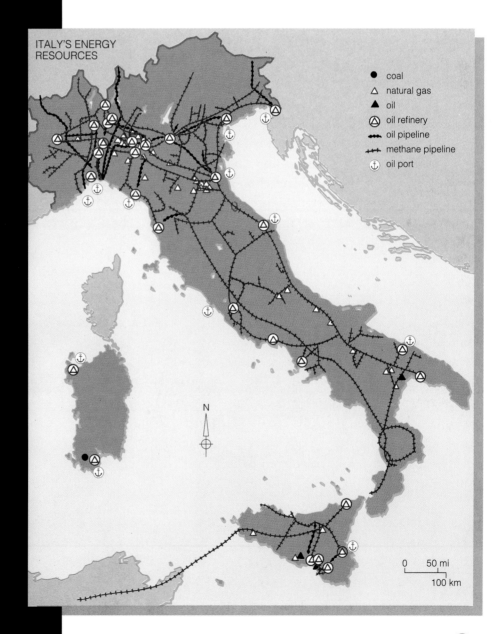

ITALY'S ENERGY
RESOURCES

● coal
△ natural gas
▲ oil
◉ oil refinery
••• oil pipeline
+++ methane pipeline
⚓ oil port

N

0   50 mi
100 km

■ POPULATION

The population of Italy is one of the highest in Europe, with 57.1 million inhabitants in 1993 – a very high figure, as more than a third of the country is mountainous. Italy is also one of Europe's most densely populated countries, with over 490 people per square mile (188 per sq km).

REGIONAL DIFFERENCES

Regional differences range from customs to languages. In Sardinia, for instance, many people speak Sardo, while Catalan is spoken by about half the inhabitants of Alghero on the island. There are also hundreds of local dialects in Italy. In 1992, it was estimated that 86% of people use both the Italian language and a dialect, while 13% can only speak in a dialect.

Italians are proud of their local traditions. Even belonging to a particular town or village can be a source of pride. This kind of loyalty is called "campanilismo" – from "campanile," or bell tower, because during

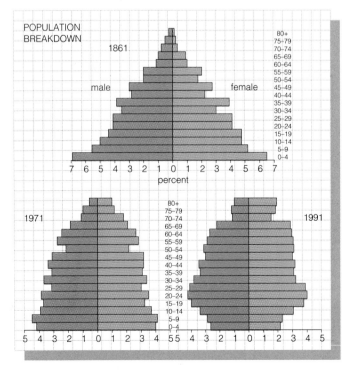

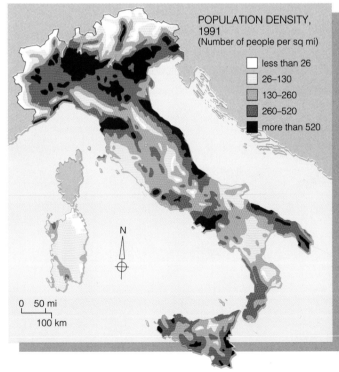

◀ *Washing day in one of the narrow, crowded streets of Naples' poorest quarter. Housing and sanitary conditions here are often extremely bad.*

▶ *A family gathering. Although Italians today have fewer children than 50 years ago, ties to extended families (grandparents, aunts, uncles, cousins, and so on) are still regarded as important.*

POPULATION GROWTH
(projected to 2000)

	1951	1961	1971	1981	1993	2000
INDIA	357,561	442,344	554,911	688,856	846,191	1,018,673
U.S.	152,271	180,671	204,879	227,722	258,233	275,326
U.K.	50,065	51,652	56,097	56,330	58,080	59,520
ITALY	47,515	50,623	54,134	56,556	57,103	57,274

(800 thousand scale; values in thousands)

KEY FACTS

● Naples is the most densely populated city in Italy, with 6,653 inhabitants per sq mi (2,559 per sq km).

● 13 of the 28 minority languages in Europe singled out in 1992 for special protection were in Italy.

● In 1992, Italy recorded the world's lowest ever birthrate: 1.2–1.3 children per woman of childbearing age.

● In 1993, 4.7% of the Italian population was aged 75 or over. This compares with 7.1% in France, 5.3% in the U.S., and 1.7% in Mexico.

● In 1994, 600,000 immigrants were estimated to be living illegally in Italy.

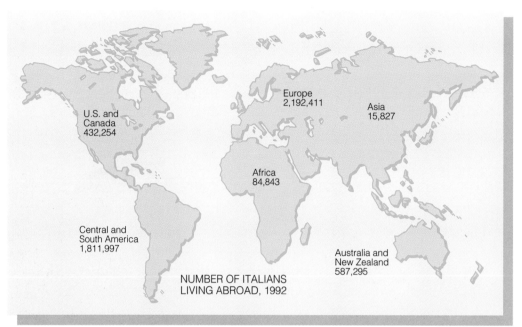

NUMBER OF ITALIANS LIVING ABROAD, 1992

U.S. and Canada 432,254

Europe 2,192,411

Asia 15,827

Africa 84,843

Central and South America 1,811,997

Australia and New Zealand 587,295

◀Between 1870 and 1970, at least 26 million Italians emigrated to seek a living abroad. This is the highest figure recorded for a European country.

the Renaissance powerful Italians demonstrated how wealthy they were by trying to build the highest bell towers in their district.

Almost every Italian town and village has its own traditions and festivals. Venice is especially famous for its annual carnival, held in the three days before Ash Wednesday. In Siena, one of the best-known festivals is the Parade of the Banner in July and August, when a horse race takes place around the main square, with riders dressed in medieval costumes.

CITY AND COUNTRYSIDE

In 1951, 52% of Italians lived in a town or city, but by 1991 the figure was 69%. The number of towns with more than 100,000

◀Immigration from North Africa (especially Morocco) has increased in recent years. Many of these newcomers are Moslems. In 1994, registered immigrants from all countries totaled 900,000.

▶People dressed in traditional costumes in a village near Monte Rosa, Piedmont.

inhabitants has risen from 22 in 1951 to 46 in 1994. However, some people are now leaving the cities for the suburbs, where houses are cheaper, the air is cleaner, and there are fewer traffic problems.

EMIGRATION AND IMMIGRATION

Emigration has become an important feature of Italian life during the 20th century. Between 1901 and 1913, as many as 8 million people, chiefly from the poorer south, left the country. This figure represented more than a fifth of Italy's total population at the time (37 million). Many emigrated to the U.S., Canada, Argentina, and Brazil.

After World War II, there was also a rapid increase in migration within Italy itself. Millions of people moved from the poorer southern and eastern regions to the north and west, where unemployment was lower and living standards were higher. Central and northern Italy account for 64.4% of the country's total population today.

Since the early 1980s, Italy has become a popular destination for immigrants from Eastern Europe and the THIRD WORLD. Many of these people settle in the larger cities, such as Milan, Rome, and Bologna. Generally, these immigrants live in poor housing areas, but, despite cultural differences, they are gradually becoming part of the new Italy.

▲ An outdoor cafe in Amalfi. The pleasant climate allows Italians to spend a great deal of their free time outside in the sunshine.

People in Italy work an average of 36 hours a week. Shops and offices often close for a long lunch break, but may stay open until 7.30 P.M. Those who work in the huge state sector — such as teachers and civil servants — usually finish work at 2 P.M., but many have a second job in the afternoons.

RELIGION

Some 98% of Italians are baptized Catholics, but only a third of them go to Sunday Mass regularly. Many just attend at Christmas and Easter. Half a million people belong to a Protestant denomination. There are also about 35,000 Jewish people in Italy, most of whom live in Rome.

The Moslem religion is becoming more important, because of immigration from North Africa. Mosques have been built in Rome, Milan, and other cities to accommodate the religious needs of these immigrants.

SPORTS AND LEISURE

Soccer is by far the most popular sport in Italy, and the country almost comes to a standstill on Sunday afternoons when

KEY FACTS

● In 1992, just over 6.5 million newspapers were sold daily in Italy, 1 million more than in 1980.
● In 1993, 40% of Italian households had a video-recorder, compared with 75% in the U.S., 59% in Germany, and 58% in France.
● Only 3% of Italians aged 15 and over are illiterate.
● Italians are big fans of car racing. Between 1952 and 1988, Ferrari Formula 1 racers won a record 93 Grand Prix races.

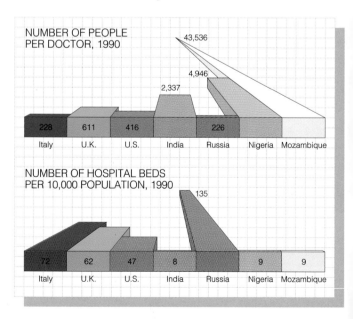

NUMBER OF PEOPLE PER DOCTOR, 1990

Italy	U.K.	U.S.	India	Russia	Nigeria	Mozambique
228	611	416	2,337	226	4,946	43,536

NUMBER OF HOSPITAL BEDS PER 10,000 POPULATION, 1990

Italy	U.K.	U.S.	India	Russia	Nigeria	Mozambique
72	62	47	8	135	9	9

league matches are played. There are 18 teams in the league's first division. Among those with the biggest followings are Juventus, from Turin, and the two Milanese teams, AC Milan and Inter Milan. Italy has won the World Cup three times, and was runner-up in 1994.

Other popular sports include car racing, cycling, skiing, tennis, basketball, and volleyball. The national volleyball team won the world title in 1994.

About 80% of Italian households have a TV set. In 1994, people watched an average of almost three and a half hours of television a day. Very few foreign-language programs are shown; instead, soap operas, movies and documentaries are virtually all dubbed. Italy's DUBBING industry is one of the biggest in the world.

Although many Italians enjoy going to the

RELIGIOUS DAYS AND HOLIDAYS

January 1	CAPODANNO (New Year's Day)
January 6	LA BEFANA (Epiphany)
March or April	PASQUETTA (Easter Monday)
April 25	ANNIVERSARIO DELLA LIBERAZIONE (Liberation Day)
May 1	PRIMO MAGGIO (Labor Day)
August 15	FERRAGOSTO (Assumption)
November 1	OGNISSANTI (All Saints' Day)
December 8	L'IMMACOLATA CONCEZIONE (Immaculate Conception)
December 25	NATALE (Christmas Day)
December 26	SANTO STEFANO (St. Stephen's Day)

▼ *The Vatican City, a separate city-state within Rome, is the home of the Roman Catholic Church, whose head is the pope.*

◄AC Milan soccer club is based at the San Siro stadium, which can hold 85,000 people. Tickets for both domestic and European matches are regularly sold out.

movies, attendance has dropped from 241 million in 1980 to 90 million in 1990. However, Italy still has an important film industry, and one of the world's most famous film festivals is held in Venice each September. Opera music is also popular in Italy, which is famous for its singers and theaters. La Scala opera house in Milan is one of the most important opera houses in the world.

EDUCATION

Schooling is compulsory and free for children between the ages of six and 14. The academic year starts in September and ends in mid-June, and there are Christmas and Easter vacations. Students do not wear school uniforms, but they must buy their own textbooks for each subject.

Children can go to a nursery school, called the "materna," when they are three years old. Between the ages of five and 11 they attend primary school, and then go to middle school until they are 14. They may leave school at this age, after taking an examination. However, most continue secondary education until they are 18. In their last year, pupils take a school leaving exam called the "maturità," a combination of written and oral tests, which they must pass if they wish to go to a university.

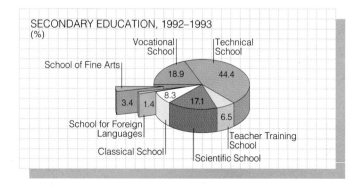

SECONDARY EDUCATION, 1992–1993
(%)

Vocational School
Technical School
School of Fine Arts
18.9
44.4
3.4 1.4 8.3 17.1
6.5
School for Foreign Languages
Classical School
Scientific School
Teacher Training School

◀*Commissioned for the cathedral in Florence, and now in the Academia, Michelangelo's famous marble statue of David was sculpted between 1501 and 1504. Other Renaissance artists include Leonardo da Vinci and Raphael. Italy's rich heritage of art and architecture dates back to before Roman times. The country's world-class museums and art galleries include the Uffizi and Pitti museums in Florence, the Vatican museum in Rome, and the Brera art gallery in Milan.*

◀*Pupils rushing home after school. The school day runs from 8 A.M. to 1:30 P.M., and children have to attend on Saturday mornings too.*

Over 1.2 million students go to universities in Italy. They must pay for this themselves, although fees are much less than in the U.K. or U.S. In the early 1990s, some universities introduced stricter admissions tests to reduce the problem of over-crowding.

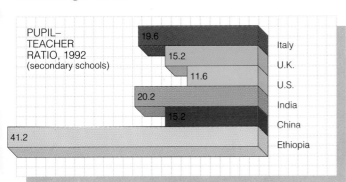

PUPIL–
TEACHER
RATIO, 1992
(secondary schools)

19.6	Italy
15.2	U.K.
11.6	U.S.
20.2	India
15.2	China
41.2	Ethiopia

■ RULES AND LAWS

After the unification of Italy in 1861, the country was ruled by a monarchy, until the rise of Fascism in 1922 meant the real power passed to the government. In 1946, Italians voted for a republican-style government, and the country officially became a democratic republic in 1948.

Parliament is Italy's legislative body. It is composed of the Chamber of Deputies (630 members) and the Senate (315 members). Although they possess identical powers, the houses meet separately to discuss and vote on legislation.

Elections are held every five years. The main political parties are the Democratic Party of the Left (PDS), Forza Italia, National Alliance (AN), and Northern League (Lega Nord).

The prime minister is appointed by the president and chooses ministers from the parties obtaining most votes in the

◀▼ A traffic policeman in Milan wears an antipollution mask, while the Polizia carry out a road check. The third police force is the Carabinieri.

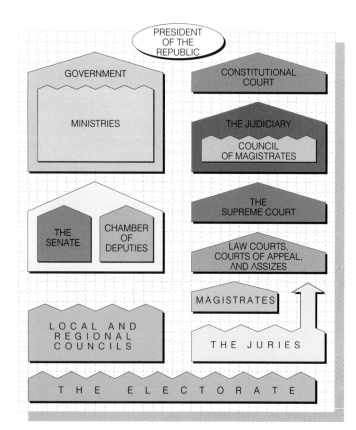

elections. These ministers make up the executive body – the government. The president, who is elected every seven years, has very few direct powers.

Regional governments representing the 20 regions are elected every five years. Further local powers are held by the provinces and communes – administrative areas governed by a council and a mayor – whose members are also elected every five years.

Citizens can vote in referendums to overturn laws. To cancel an existing law, at least 50% of those eligible must vote. Proposals to make hunting illegal in a referendum in 1990 failed because not enough people turned out to vote.

KEY FACTS

● At the age of 18, all Italian men are eligible for 9 months' military service, although they may choose community work instead.
● There has been no death penalty in Italy since 1946, but soldiers may theoretically be executed for disobedience during wartime.
● No less than 54 governments were formed between 1945 and 1995.
● Defense spending in Italy amounts to 2.4% of the national budget. The world average is 4.9%.
● There are 680 people to each police officer in Italy, compared with 345 in the U.S., 420 in the U.K., and 1,360 in China.
● Almost 200 members of Parliament were investigated for involvement in the bribes scandal which came to light in 1992–94.

▲ *Suspected* MAFIA *criminals behind bars erected inside the courtroom during a recent trial. There are three organized crime networks in Italy: the Cosa Nostra, based in Sicily; the 'ndrangheta in Calabria; and the Camorra in Campania. The Mafia is still a powerful threat to the country's institutions.*

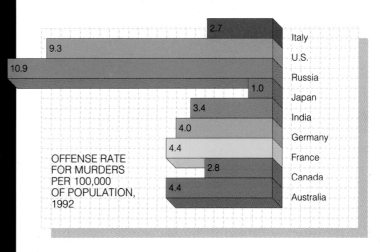

OFFENSE RATE FOR MURDERS PER 100,000 OF POPULATION, 1992

Italy	2.7
U.S.	9.3
Russia	10.9
Japan	1.0
India	3.4
Germany	4.0
France	4.4
Canada	2.8
Australia	4.4

FOOD AND FARMING

Since so much of Italy is mountainous or hilly, in many areas farming is a difficult business. However, since the 1960s farming has become more mechanized. Larger farms have been set up, especially in the north.

The chief cereal crop is wheat. The common wheat crop used for bread is grown mainly in the north, while 75% of the harder durum wheat used for pasta is grown in the south. Corn is Italy's second most important crop, and small quantities of oats and barley are also grown in the south. Excellent-quality rice is found mostly in the western regions of the Po Valley. In 1992, production rose to 1.4 million tons, more than half the European total.

Grapes are cultivated all over the country, especially in the southern regions of Puglia and Sicily. Many wines are exported, particularly to the United States, France, and Germany. Olives are grown chiefly in the sunnier southern regions. Together with Spain, Italy is the world's leading producer of olive oil, yielding a total of 600,000 tons a year.

Apricots, figs, and citrus fruits such as oranges and lemons are grown principally

◀ *An Italian delicatessen may sell salami, olive oil, fresh spices, sauces, and a variety of pastas and breads.*

▶ *Fish and seafood form the basis of many popular dishes, such as grilled swordfish, or spaghetti served with little clams.*

THE MAIN CROPS

- pasture and woods
- mixed farmland
- cereals
- fruit and olives
- ⤫ fishing

N

0   50 mi

100 km

KEY FACTS

● In 1990, 28% of agricultural workers in Italy were aged 65 or more.

● In 1991, agriculture accounted for just 3.3% of national income, compared with 28% in 1950 and 50% in 1900.

● Italy's fishing catch in 1991 amounted to 355,000 tons, compared with 3.3 million for the U.S., and 1.3 million for Spain.

● Each Italian eats an average of 63 pounds (29 kg) of meat a year, compared with a European average of 50 pounds (23 kg), and a U.S. average of 110 pounds (50 kg).

in the south. Central and northern regions produce apples, cherries, peaches, and pears. The most important fruit or vegetable is the tomato: 6 million tons are grown each year, chiefly in the central-southern regions.

Fishing is still an important industry. Varieties such as sardines, mackerel, and anchovies are the most widely fished specimens, especially in the Adriatic. Swordfish are common around Calabria. Mollusks and crustaceans, such as clams, squid, and shrimps, are found everywhere and account for 50% of the total fishing catch.

Italians eat a great deal of beef, pork, and chicken, but much of the meat is imported. The north is the most important area for raising pigs and cattle, while

▲ *Year-round mild temperatures make Sicily an ideal location for growing oranges. It accounts for 66% of Italy's citrus fruit production and is the world's chief producer of lemons.*

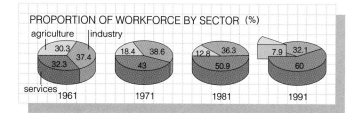

PROPORTION OF WORKFORCE BY SECTOR (%)

agriculture | industry

	1961	1971	1981	1991
agriculture	30.3	18.4	12.8	7.9
industry	37.4	38.6	36.3	32.1
services	32.3	43	50.9	60

▲ *Cheese-making in progress. Famous Italian cheeses include Parmesan, gorgonzola, and mozzarella.*

▲ *Parmesan cheeses are stored on wooden racks. Experts tap them with a wooden hammer to test their quality.*

sheep and goats are raised in central-southern regions and the islands. Italy is famous for the production of salami, most of which comes from Emilia Romagna.

Food specialities can vary from town to town. They include Neapolitan pizzas, Florentine steaks, and Bolognese pasta dishes. In the north, you can try RISOTTO with "porcini" mushrooms, or POLENTA, a kind of thick porridge, with sausage or inkfish stew.

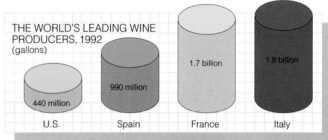

THE WORLD'S LEADING WINE PRODUCERS, 1992 (gallons)

U.S.	Spain	France	Italy
440 million	990 million	1.7 billion	1.8 billion

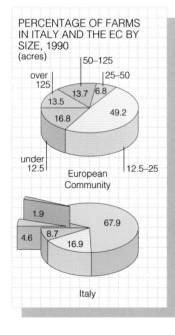

PERCENTAGE OF FARMS IN ITALY AND THE EC BY SIZE, 1990 (acres)

European Community
- over 125: 13.5
- 50–125: 13.7
- 25–50: 6.8
- 12.5–25: 49.2
- under 12.5: 16.8

Italy
- 1.9
- 4.6
- 8.7
- 16.9
- 67.9

▶ *Chianti, the famous red wine, is produced from Canaiolo grapes in Tuscany.*

TRADE AND INDUSTRY

Despite a lack of natural resources, Italy experienced an industrial boom in the 1950s and 1960s, and is now one of the most highly industrialized countries in the world. Industry is concentrated in the north of the country, but efforts are being made to industrialize the more agricultural south.

TRADING PARTNERS

Italy's chief trading partners are other European countries, accounting for 73.9% of imports and 72.4% of exports in 1992. The figures for North America were 8.4% and 10.5% respectively, while Asian markets provided 9.9% of imports and took 11.9% of exports.

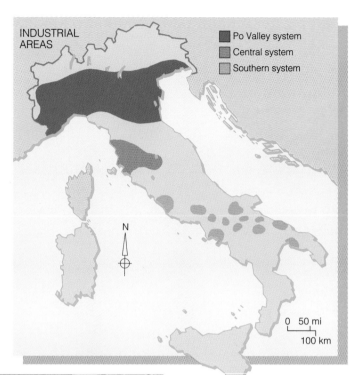

INDUSTRIAL AREAS

- Po Valley system
- Central system
- Southern system

N

0   50 mi
100 km

KEY FACTS

● In 1992, the area around Sassuolo accounted for 74% of national ceramic tile production. Italy leads the world in this, with 27% of the market.
● Only 8 of the world's leading multinational companies are Italian.
● Italy is the world's leader in the export of tomato paste, valued at 779 billion lire in 1991.
● In 1992, the Olivetti company sold 700,000 personal computers – the highest figure for any European company.

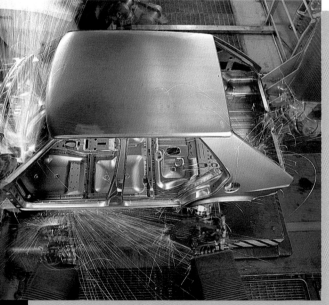

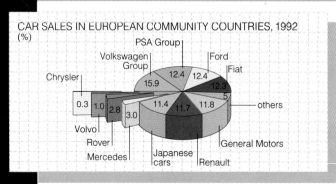

CAR SALES IN EUROPEAN COMMUNITY COUNTRIES, 1992 (%)

PSA Group
Volkswagen Group
Ford
Fiat
Chrysler
12.4   12.4
15.9   12.3
5
0.3   1.0   2.8   3.0   11.4   11.7   11.8   others
Volvo
Rover
Mercedes
Japanese cars
Renault
General Motors

◄In 1993, Fiat opened a new car factory in Melfi, near Picenza. Robots help achieve production of 1,800 cars a day.

►Ferrari is famous for its luxury sports cars and Formula 1 racing cars. Fewer than 4,000 road cars were produced in the 1980s, when the price of a car topped $100,000.

SUCCESSFUL INDUSTRIES

Much of Italy's success is due to the vitality of small and medium-sized companies situated mostly in the north and center of the country. No less than 77% of industrial production is accounted for by companies employing less than 20 people each. Most of these manufacturing companies are equipped with modern technology.

The creation of several hundred industrial districts specializing in the manufacture of a single product has proved highly successful. Chiefly based in the north, these districts were set up during the 1970s and are composed of a network of small companies sharing information and technology and a common marketing

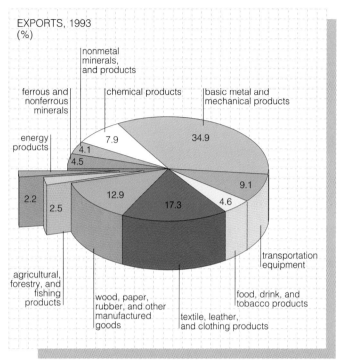

EXPORTS, 1993 (%)

nonmetal minerals, and products

ferrous and nonferrous minerals

chemical products 7.9

basic metal and mechanical products 34.9

energy products 4.1

4.5

2.2

2.5

12.9

17.3

9.1

4.6

transportation equipment

agricultural, forestry, and fishing products

wood, paper, rubber, and other manufactured goods

textile, leather, and clothing products

food, drink, and tobacco products

◀ *The Regatta Storica, held each September along the Grand Canal in Venice, dates back seven centuries. Sights like this bring millions of tourists to Italy each year.*

strategy. Among the most famous are the districts of Empoli (glass), Carpi (woolens), Brianza (furniture), Vigevano (shoes), and Sassuolo (tiles).

Also concentrated in the north, the country's mechanical industry is important across the world. The car industry is perhaps the best known. Manufacturers include Fiat, based in Turin, which secured 4.5% of the world market in 1992, while Ferrari, Maserati, and Lamborghini aim for a wealthier market. Apart from cars, the country's machine tools industry –

manufacturing equipment for other industries – is also significant. In 1992, this sector of Italian industry was the world's third largest, after Japan and Germany.

Other highly successful industries include agricultural machinery, household appliances, and high-precision instruments, such as periscopes, microscopes, and navigational equipment. Italy is also the world's fourth biggest exporter of arms.

IRON AND STEEL INDUSTRY

Previously forming one of Italy's leading industries, the iron and steel works in the north and along the coast are now closing down because of competition from third world countries and a drop in demand. Nevertheless, Italy is the sixth most important producer of steel in the world today, accounting for 3.3% of global production. In Europe it is second only to Germany. The country is also the world's leading producer of special steels,

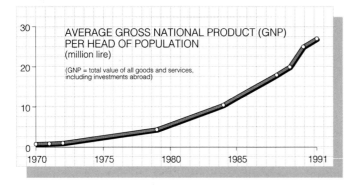

AVERAGE GROSS NATIONAL PRODUCT (GNP) PER HEAD OF POPULATION (million lire)

(GNP = total value of all goods and services, including investments abroad)

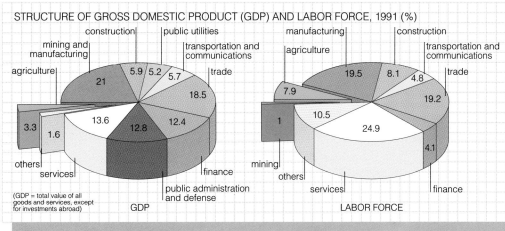

STRUCTURE OF GROSS DOMESTIC PRODUCT (GDP) AND LABOR FORCE, 1991 (%)

construction
public utilities
mining and manufacturing
transportation and communications
agriculture
trade
5.9 5.2 5.7
21
18.5
3.3
13.6
12.8
12.4
1.6
others
services
public administration and defense
finance

(GDP = total value of all goods and services, except for investments abroad)
GDP

manufacturing
construction
agriculture
transportation and communications
trade
19.5
8.1
4.8
7.9
19.2
1
10.5
24.9
4.1
mining
others
services
finance

LABOR FORCE

Gianni Versace and his models on a catwalk during a fashion show in Milan. Exports of Italian clothes were valued at 23,000 billion lire in 1992.

containing metals such as tungsten and nickel, which are used in the manufacture of tools and special heat-resistant products for the naval and aeronautics industries.

CLOTHING AND TOURISM

Italian clothing designers such as Armani, Benetton, Versace, and Valentino are famous everywhere. Fashion shows in Milan and Florence attract people from all over the world. The country exports immense quantities of shoes, clothes, leather goods, and eyeglasses. More than 1.15 million people were employed in Italy's clothing industry in 1992.

Italy is also one of the world's most visited countries. Many tourists come to view its great cultural and artistic heritage, while others are attracted by the climate and scenery. The most-visited regions are the Veneto and Trentino-Alto Adige in the northeast of the country, and Emilia Romagna, and Tuscany in northern-central Italy.

Just over 19% of the working population is involved in tourism. In 1990 more than 59 million people visited the country. Income from tourism totaled $19,688 million in 1991.

▼ *A shipyard in Naples. Apart from the pleasure-boat sector, Italy's shipbuilding industry is currently in crisis, because other countries, such as Japan, produce ships much more cheaply.*

TRANSPORTATION

◄ *Soccer fans climbing aboard a streetcar in Milan. Since the late 1980s, this romantic form of transportation has become more popular in Italy's overcrowded cities, since streetcars produce much less pollution than automobiles or buses.*

Ever since the industrial boom of the 1950s and 1960s, Italy's government has given priority to the development of an efficient highway network, which has helped to boost trade, car sales, and tourism. A toll highway links east to west in the north (Trieste-Milan-Turin) and there are two highways linking north to south. Firstly, along the Tyrrhenian coast, the "autostrada del sole" (highway of the sun) connects Milan to Reggio di Calabria before proceeding to Catania and Palermo in Sicily. At 776 miles (1,250 km), it is Italy's longest and most important highway. The second major route links Milan to Bari via Ancona. Other routes from east to west remain underdeveloped because of the Apennine mountain range in the center of the country.

More than half the 11,800 miles (19,000 km) of the country's railroad network has been electrified. In 1990, a high-speed train called

the "pendolino" was introduced, cutting travel time between Rome and Milan (384 miles [640 km]) to four hours. Other high-speed trains are to follow.

The three major airports – Fiumicino in Rome and Linate and Malpensa in Milan – account for 62% of passenger traffic and 85% of cargo traffic. The lack of space near major cities, and poor road and rail links between airports and cities, have hampered development. But air travel has grown rapidly since the mid-1970s.

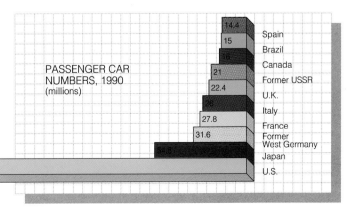

PASSENGER CAR NUMBERS, 1990 (millions)

Spain	14.4
Brazil	15
Canada	16
Former USSR	21
U.K.	22.4
Italy	26
France	27.8
Former West Germany	31.6
Japan	34.8
U.S.	186

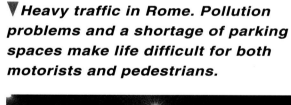

▲ *A highway exit near Genoa. Engineers have had to use a lot of skill to solve problems caused by mountainous land and lack of space.*

▼ *Heavy traffic in Rome. Pollution problems and a shortage of parking spaces make life difficult for both motorists and pedestrians.*

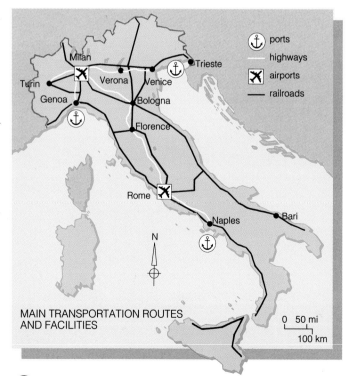

⚓ ports
highways
✈ airports
── railroads

Milan
Turin
Genoa
Verona
Venice
Trieste
Bologna
Florence
Rome
Naples
Bari

N

MAIN TRANSPORTATION ROUTES
AND FACILITIES

0 50 mi
100 km

KEY FACTS

- Italy's underground train network totals 618 miles (103 km), compared with 454 miles (756 km) in the U.K.
- Italy's highway network is the third most extensive in the world, after those in the U.S. and Germany.
- In 1994, 83% of goods transported in Italy went by road.
- The speed limit on Italian highways is 72 mph (120 kph).
- Crude oil makes up 60% of the goods imported by sea.

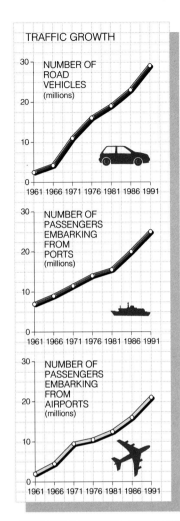

TRAFFIC GROWTH

NUMBER OF ROAD VEHICLES (millions)

NUMBER OF PASSENGERS EMBARKING FROM PORTS (millions)

NUMBER OF PASSENGERS EMBARKING FROM AIRPORTS (millions)

Transportation by water is a slower but cheaper alternative, especially for transporting goods. For reasons of cost, people traveling to Sicily, Sardinia, and Elba tend to use ferries rather than airplanes. There are also 900 miles (1,500 km) of navigable rivers and 510 miles (850 km) of canals, but they are not fully used.

Because of the priority given to developing roads, public transportation systems in Italy have been relatively neglected. In 1991, 71% of urban traffic consisted of private cars. In 1993, over 28 million cars were on the road in Italy, and for every car there were 1.9 people – compared with a EUROPEAN UNION (formerly "European Community") average of three people per car.

▼ *Alitalia jets on the runway at Linate airport in Milan. Set up in 1947, the national airline now has a modern fleet of more than 120 planes.*

THE ENVIRONMENT

Spiaggia infetta vacanza perfetta.

tutti gli inquinamenti fini... o in mar... ...Cousteau

IL MARE MUORE

◀ *Antipollution protesters on the march along the Adriatic coast. Local people try to ensure that beaches are kept clean in order to attract tourists.*

▼ *Smog has become a big problem in cities such as Milan.*

NUMBER OF CARS PER SQ MILE, 1990

France	84.5
Germany	154
U.S.	110.8
Italy	208.3

In the process of industrialization, Italy built thousands of factories, refineries, and industrial plants. During the 1950s and 1960s, there were few controls on building, and huge areas of land and coastline were cleared. Some plant and animal life disappeared. Italy's great architectural heritage has also been severely damaged by pollution. People are more concerned about these problems today.

Disposal of industrial waste and household trash are two major problems. Municipal dumps are full, and so are unable to cope with increasing quantities of household waste. Since the mid-1980s, local councils have made limited attempts to cope with the problem by installing special containers to recycle paper, glass, and plastic. About 75 million tons of toxic waste are produced annually by factories and industries. As industrial waste dumps are also full, 70% of this dangerous material is disposed of in illegal dumps, or exported.

Air pollution caused by factory fumes, heating systems, and cars is another problem. At certain times, cities like Milan, Turin, Naples, and Rome are forced to close off their centers to private traffic to reduce the amount of toxic fumes in the air.

Water pollution means that the aquifer (the soil and rock layers through which water filters) in some areas of the Po Valley is now so badly affected that drinking water

◀*Gran Paradiso national park in Valle d'Aosta covers 175,000 acres (70,000 ha).*

PERCENTAGE OF
NATIONAL TERRITORY
UNDER PROTECTION, 1992

31 Denmark	**22** U.K.
20 Germany	**18** Austria
14 Japan	**13** Australia
10 New Zealand	**9** U.S.
8 Hungary	**7** Switzerland
6 France	**2** Italy
1 Spain	**1** Greece

national parks
regional parks
● nature reserves and
protected areas
● marine parks

N

NATIONAL PARKS
AND RESERVES

0   50 mi
0   100 km

supplies have been contaminated. In 1986, about 400,000 people in the area had no drinking water after it was found to contain weedkillers. In Piedmont, part of the Bormida River was declared biologically dead in 1993 as a result of illegal chemical dumping.

Seawater pollution is extensive too. Much of the sewage and waste dumped in the Po

▶*A member of the squirrel family, the marmot inhabits open country in the Alps. Strict hunting restrictions imposed by the government have ensured the animals' survival.*

▼*Battery recycling bins made their appearance all over Italy at the end of the 1980s.*

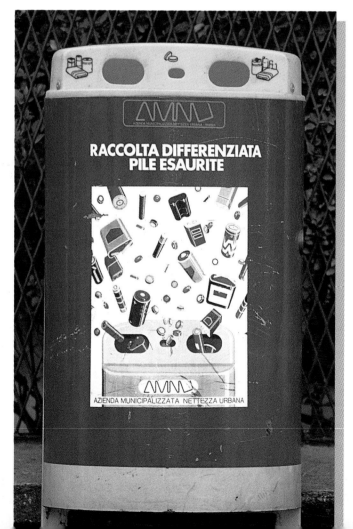

Valley waterways ends up in the upper Adriatic Sea to the east. Large, evil-smelling mats of algae (seaweed and other water plants) have formed in the Adriatic every summer since 1989. Occasional oil spills from gasoline tankers and the illegal dumping of industrial waste in the sea also create pollution.

Public pressure to improve the threatened environment has led to the creation of more green areas in cities. A recent trend has seen private companies sponsoring plans aimed at improving and conserving such areas. Moreover, as a result of campaigning by groups like the Environment League and Italia Nostra ("Our Italy"), building projects are now regulated more carefully.

National parks and reserves have been established to preserve natural areas from destruction and to save animals from the risk of extinction. Between 1988 and 1991, two new national reserves were created in the Valgrande near Lake Maggiore, and in the Dolomites in the northeast of the country. A Ministry for the Environment was set up in 1986, and several laws governing the environment have been issued at European level.

▼ *Two male ibex sparring in the Italian Alps. These mountain goats live along the permanent snow line. Once common, the ibex is now a protected species in Italy.*

KEY FACTS

● In 1990, the city with the highest sulfur dioxide level in the world was Milan.
● Only 5% of the 20 million tons of waste produced each year in Italy is recycled.
● Despite major efforts to clean up beaches, in 1992 it was estimated that 25% of the Italian coastline was unsuitable for swimming.
● The amount of land damaged as a result of fire rose from 475,000 acres (190,000 ha) in 1985 to 517,500 acres (207,000 ha) in 1993.
● In 1991, the Italian government passed a law specifying maximum noise levels in inhabited areas.
● Hunting is still a popular pastime. In 1989, 1.5 million people applied for a hunting permit.

THE FUTURE

Italy is experiencing a period of great economic, social, and political change. National prosperity is not evenly spread across the country, as the poorer regions in the south still lag behind their northern and central neighbors. The government is attempting to remedy this by providing economic assistance. Private companies investing in the south are granted tax breaks and favorable financial terms. Investments in the service industries, tourism, and research companies hold the key to success in this area, although the Mafia remains a problem to be defeated.

The falling birth rate in Italy is creating concern. On current trends, the number of retired people will soon outnumber those in the workforce. Politicians and economists are currently working out a new pension plan to ensure that the workers of today will have decent pensions in the future.

Technology plays an important role in the daily lives of Italians, as computers and fax machines are increasingly used at home and at work. This means more people are deciding to move away from their place of work in the cities to work at home. Another recent development is that, in collaboration with schools and universities, companies are establishing new scientific parks and technology research centers called

KEY FACTS

● On current trends, Italy's population will decline to 44 million in 2025 – the same figure as in the 1930s.
● Approximately 40% of Italian men and 60% of Italian women can now expect to live to the age of 80.
● Italian companies such as Fiat are expanding their know-how into the ex-Eastern European bloc to ensure future markets and profits.
● Architects have plans to build "cities of the future" in Milan and Turin, including underground factories and roads, and an overhead railroad system.

▲ *Situated near Turin, the Olivetti-based "technocity" provides work and research facilities.*

◄ *Begun in 1174 and completed during the 14th century, the Leaning Tower of Pisa is 181.5 feet (55 m) tall. Part of the tower has sunk into the soft ground on which it was built, and over the years it has developed a 16 foot (5 m) "tilt." Engineers have recently tried to shore up the foundations with cement, but must find new techniques to prevent the tower from collapsing. Italy also needs to preserve other historical monuments which have been damaged by pollution.*

"technocities." Major centers have been set up in Milan, Turin, and Bari.

Given its geographical position, Italy hopes to establish itself as a link between Europe, Africa, and the Middle East. It is already a key member of international groups, as it has been part of both the European Union (EU), formerly the European Community (EC), and the Western military alliance, NATO (North Atlantic Treaty Organization), since they were set up. Despite differences within the country, Italians are enthusiastic about the EU and look forward to playing an active role in its future.

FURTHER INFORMATION

● ALITALIA AIRLINE
666 Fifth Avenue, New York, N.Y 10100
● ITALIAN EMBASSY
1601 Fuller Street, N.W., Washington,
D.C. 20009
● ITALIAN TOURIST OFFICE
530 Fifth Avenue, New York, N.Y 10020

BOOKS ABOUT ITALY
Angelillo, Barbara W. *Italy*, "World in View"
   series. Raintree Steck-Vaughn, 1991
Borlenghi, Patricia and Wright, Rachel.
   Italy. Watts, 1993
Travis, David. *The Land and People of Italy*.
   HarperCollins, 1992
Wright, David and Wright, Jill. *Italy*.
   Trafalgar Square, 1991
Wright, Nicola. *Getting to Know Italy and
   Italian*. Barron, 1993

GLOSSARY

BORA
A strong wind which blows across north-
eastern Italy.

DEMOCRACY
A country in which the people rule, usually
through elected representatives.

DUBBING
Providing a movie with a new sound track in
a different language from the original.

EUROPEAN UNION
Known as the European Community until
1994, an organization of European nations
formed with the aim of establishing common
defense, trading, social, political, foreign,
and economic policies.

FASCISM
A type of government where one person
has absolute power and individual freedoms
are restricted. Italy had a fascist
government, led by Benito Mussolini, from
1922 to 1943.

MAFIA
A secret criminal society, originating in
Sicily, which controls many illegal activities.

MEZZOGIORNO
The economically underdeveloped area of
southern and southeastern Italy, including
Sicily and Sardinia.

PENINSULA
A narrow strip of land projecting from the
mainland into a sea, ocean, or lake.

POLENTA
A type of thick porridge or mush, usually
made of cornmeal.

RENAISSANCE
The period in European history from the
14th to 16th centuries, when interest in
ancient Greek and Roman works was
reawakened, and art and learning
flourished.

RISOTTO
A dish of rice cooked with meat, onions,
and other vegetables.

THIRD WORLD
The underdeveloped countries of the world.

INDEX

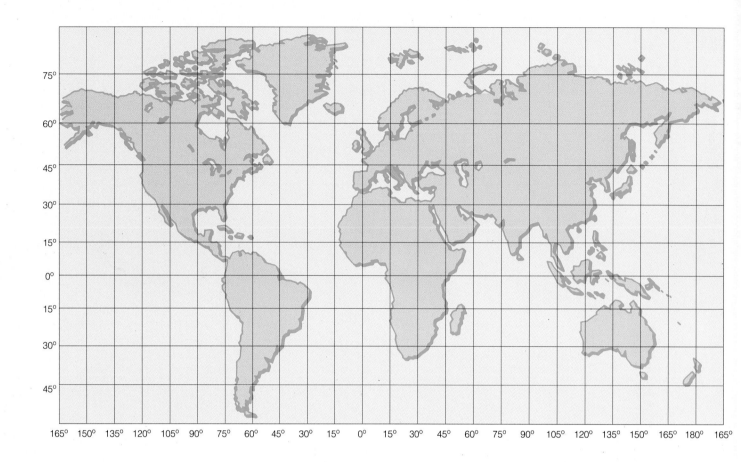